the everywhere
Bear

Written by
Sandra Chisholm
Robinson

Designed by
Gail Kohler Opsahl

Illustrated by
The Denver Museum
of Natural History

The Wonder Series

Denver Museum of Natural History
and Roberts Rinehart Publishers

Published in the United States of America by
Roberts Rinehart Publishers, Post Office Box 666,
Niwot, Colorado 80544.

Published in Great Britain, Ireland, and Europe by
Roberts Rinehart Publishers, 3 Bayview Terrace,
Schull, West Cork, Republic of Ireland.

Published in Canada by Key Porter Books,
70 The Esplanade, Toronto, Ontario M5E 1R2.

Library of Congress Catalog Card Number
91-66678

International Standard Book Number
1-879373-07-6

Manufactured in the United States of America.

Thank you

to the following people for the time and knowledge they have given to *The Everywhere Bear:* Gary Brown, Bear Management Specialist; Stan Osolinski and Jeff Henry, wildlife photographers; and George Robinson, Chief Naturalist for Yellowstone National Park. Judge Robert Crew first got us thinking about dreaming bears. Thanks, also, to the students of the fourth grade class of Kathy Tullis, Irving School, Bozeman, Montana, for their comments and drawings. And special thanks to my son, Garrett, whose sense of humor gets us through the deadlines.

—Sandra Chisholm Robinson

The Wonder Series

the everywhere
Bear

Decorate this page

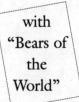

with "Bears of the World"

stickers!

See page 16...

CONTENTS

Introduction

Bears are everywhere!

Paddington® Bears, Care Bears®, and Smokey Bear dance across our wallpaper, decorate our mugs and plates, hold our toothbrushes, keep us safe in bed at night, and invite us from the pages of books to join their adventures. Our favorite bears are not just earthbound. Look up! Bears are in the sky. The "star bears," Ursa major ("Great Bear") and Ursa minor ("Little Bear"), are known as the Big Dipper and Little Dipper.

Everyone loves stuffed bears, storybook bears, and star bears, but what about real bears? Would you snuggle beneath the bed covers with a real grizzly bear? Would an honest-to-goodness black bear sit quietly for an afternoon tea and honey party? Probably not!

Three kinds of real bears live in North America: *Ursus arctos,* the grizzly; *Ursus americanus,* the black bear; and *Ursus maritimus,* the polar bear. Eight species of bears live throughout the world (including North America).

People have different feelings about real bears. Ask 10 people, "How do you feel about bears?" You will likely hear a variety of responses. Humans often have mixed emotions about bears. They use words such as loveable, vicious, cute, funny, dangerous, and lazy.

Meanwhile, digging for roots, scrounging whitebark pine nuts from a squirrel's midden, and tasting the air for the first big snow that will seal its den for the winter, the bear is unaware of our feelings. However, human attitudes are affecting the survival of bears throughout the world. The bear cannot change who it is. But we humans can change our attitudes and actions.

How important is it to have bears in your world? Over 60 years ago, the famous American poet, Robert Frost wrote: "The world has room to make a bear feel free."

Does the world still have room for both people and bears?

Nowhere for the Everywhere Bear

The game includes:

- The puzzle pieces on this page
- The story, "Nowhere for the Everywhere Bear," on pages 7 to 9
- The answer key on page 63

You need:

- Crayons, color pencils, or fine tip markers
- Scissors

Before playing:

- Remove this page from the book.
- Color, then cut out the puzzle pieces along the dashed lines.

Objective:

- To complete the puzzle by reading the story.

To play:

1. Place the puzzle pieces around you.
2. Read the story and build the puzzle step-by-step. The directions are in the story.

After playing:

To play again, save the puzzle pieces in an envelope. Tape the envelope into your book. Or you may paste the completed puzzle onto your own piece of paper and make an Everywhere Bear poster!

Nowhere for the Everywhere Bear

The bear sniffed, and then sniffed again. The flavor of the air had changed.

The bear yawned, scratched behind his softly rounded ear with his claws, turned over in the snug confines of his den, and settled back to sleep. But his thoughts turned to ripe carcasses; fat, starchy roots; green juicy plants; plump purple berries; and oily, crunchy nuts. Perhaps the time had come to get up after all!

The bear was slow and sleepy after six months in hibernation. He dug away the thin layer of snow that sealed his den, and thrust himself into the world. After months of darkness, the bear blinked his eyes against the startling brightness. He sat on his haunches in the snow and warmed himself, his black fur turning the sun's light into heat. The bear fell over in the warmth, curled up, and thought about going back to sleep. But the smells, the sounds, and the movement of a world waking up produced an excitement and an urgency in the bear's belly.

Although the bear had not eaten a bite in months, he was not ravenously hungry. He was a healthy bear with a soft, fatty paunch. Although the smell of spring was in the air, it was still winter where the bear had denned. The bear's mother had been a good teacher; the young bear had learned to make his den between tree roots on the side of the mountain that was sheltered from the wind. If the bear had chosen the other side of the mountain to make his den, the snow that insulated the chamber would have been blown away. The bear would have been exposed to winter weather in the harshest and most bitter time of the year.

For a while, sleeping in day beds, the bear remained in the area of his den. Then his belly decided it was time to move on. Vacation was over! The bear must begin making a "bear living"—finding food!

In some part of himself, the bear remembered a place of food, a carcass. As his body recuperated from the long, inactive winter, his stomach began to growl. A meal of meat would satisfy his hunger. The bear shook himself and followed his memory.

Finally the bear stood at the edge of a forest. He studied the meadow before him. The bear had moved from the deep snow of the mountains to a place of green pasture. Here only patchy snow remained, a lingering reminder to humans and their animals that spring and summer were brief, and that winter always came too soon.

The animals in the pasture moved about slowly. Cared for by humans, they had lost the caution of wild creatures. The bear sniffed a carcass and, moving carefully, left the protection of the forest. The bear bit into the frozen meat, but the growl in his belly was muffled by a sound like thunder. The bear yelped as he felt the bullet's sting. Hunger forgotten, the bear ran for the safety of the trees.

Now far from the heavy, slow moving creatures, the bear licked the fur on his rump. He had only been grazed, the wound would heal quickly. But this was nowhere for the Everywhere Bear. Was it?

Find the first piece of the puzzle. It pictures the scene you just read about.

The hunger returned, and with it another memory—a stream that passed through a low, gentle valley with tender, moist plants. The Everywhere Bear followed his memory.

The bear sniffed the air, and retreated. His stomach growled. He took a few steps forward, but the smell on the wind made the bear turn away. The bear could respond only to the scent in his nose, and his wild caution served him well. Spring came early to the low valley; there was clear, tumbling water with young plants growing at the stream's edge. But what the bear loved, humans loved. Wildflowers would not bloom in the valley this spring. The dirt was broken and turned. Instead of wildflowers, houses for humans sprouted in the valley. This place was nowhere for the Everywhere Bear. Was it?

Place the second piece of the puzzle next to the first.

The bear followed the trail of the sun. He felt the days lengthen. His hunger grew. The bear gave in to a strong, rank odor he smelled in the dry air. He was not alone as he rummaged through the leavings of another animal. But dogs barked, car doors slammed, people yelled, and finally the small bear was run off by bigger bears. A garbage dump was nowhere for the Everywhere Bear. Was it?

Place the third piece into the puzzle.

The bear turned again to the mountain. There he would find berries, meadows of roots and tubers, and sometimes the bonus of a vole or a ground squirrel dug up with the herbs. The bear placed his feet in deep tracks made by bears that had passed before for many years. But now there were other tracks; tracks that ran unbroken for miles, tracks that changed the natural patterns of the mountain. The barely ripe berries were squashed in the tracks. The human animal dug deep in the earth and took its riches, its oil and gold, its thermal waters. Again the bear turned away; the noise and the smoke of people digging was nowhere for the Everywhere Bear. Was it?

Place the fourth piece into the puzzle.

With each passing year the circle tightens. Moving among grazing lands; housing developments; campgrounds; ski resorts; and oil, mineral, and thermal exploration; the bear follows his hunger and his memories. Only people can decide to save wilderness lands—to share with the Everywhere Bear.

Fit the Everywhere Bear piece into the puzzle.

Is there somewhere for the Everywhere Bear?

Spirit Bear

When you see this sign in the book, find the sticker with the picture that matches the description. Paste the sticker over the Spirit Bear. These stickers show the many ways that American Indians relate to the bear.

Key on page 63.

Bears of the World

What is happening with the bears of the world?

Eight species of bears live throughout the world. Two species appear to be fairly stable. The other six, however, are in trouble.

Who or what is causing the bears' decline?

People.

Why?

The activities of humans are depriving all species of bears of their natural **habitat**.

What activities?

People are destroying bear habitat by clearing land for farming, timber harvest, oil and gas exploration, and development. People are killing individual bears to protect their property and to make money from selling bear parts.

Bears throughout the world have already lost one-half to three-quarters of their original range! According to biologist Christopher Servheen, "the fate of bears in many areas of the world will be decided in the next 10 to 20 years."

American Black Bear
(Ursus americanus)

DISTRIBUTION
In North America, the bears most people are familiar with are American black bears. These bears live in the forests of Canada, northern Mexico, and 32 states in the United States.

HABITAT
Forests and meadows.

SIZE
125-350 pounds (60-160 kg), 4-6 feet long (1.2-1.8 m).

FOOD HABITS
The black bear's diet varies depending on location and season, but usually includes berries, nuts, carrion (dead animals), fish, insects, grass and herbs, honey, moose calves (Alaska), and lemmings (northern Canada).

STATUS
American black bears are now being killed in large numbers to supply people in Asia with bear parts, because Asiatic black bears, sun and sloth bears have become rare.

In the western United States, black bear populations are quite high in many areas.

BROWN BEARS *(Ursus arctos)*

Brown bears have the greatest geographic range of any bear. They live in Europe, Asia, and western North America. There are two American subspecies:

Grizzly Bear *(Ursus arctos horribilus)*

SIZE

300-600 pounds (135-270 kg), 6-8 feet (1.8-2.4 m) long.

DISTRIBUTION

The grizzly bear lives in western North America. In the United States, the grizzly lives in Alaska, Wyoming, Montana, Idaho, and Washington.

Kodiak Bear *(Ursus arctos middendorffi)*

SIZE

400-600 pounds (180-270 kg) (a large male may weigh 1,500 pounds [680 kg]), 9 feet long (2.7 m). Kodiak bears are thought to be the largest brown bears in the world.

DISTRIBUTION

This bear lives on three Alaskan islands.

HABITAT

Tundra, forests, meadows, and along coastlines.

FOOD HABITS

Brown bear diets vary, but may include salmon, trout, mollusks, crabs, moose calves, deer, elk, caribou, fruits, berries, roots and herbs, and carrion.

STATUS

Throughout their range, the habitat of brown bears continues to shrink because of human activities. Brown bears also reproduce slowly and many cubs die. Before 1800, 50,000 to 100,000 grizzlies lived in the lower 48 states. Today less than 1,000 grizzlies live in four western states. In Alaska, Canada, and Russia, grizzlies and other brown bears have more stable populations, but they, too, are affected by human activities.

Polar Bear *(Ursus maritimus)*

DISTRIBUTION

A polar bear could be called the bear that sits on top of the world. Its home is the frozen wilderness of the Arctic.

HABITAT

Polar bears are bears of the sea (*maritimus* means "sea"). Although the bear may walk great distances, it often catches a ride on a piece of ice to hunt migrating seals.

SIZE

660-1300 pounds (300-590 kg), 8-11.5 feet (2.4-3.5 m) long.

FOOD HABITS

Polar bears eat ringed seals, bearded seals, walruses, carrion (dead whales, fish, and so forth), rodents, reindeer, and berries.

STATUS

When Eskimos using traditional weapons and methods hunted polar bears, they did not endanger the bear population. Europeans came to the Arctic with guns. By the 1960s, polar bears were nearly wiped out in parts of their range. In 1967, the five "polar bear nations" of Canada, Norway, Russia, Sweden, and the United States agreed to either stop or control hunting. Although the polar bear is currently not in danger of extinction, many problems still exist.

Sun Bear *(Ursus malayanus)*

DISTRIBUTION

Sun bears live in several countries in southeast Asia.

HABITAT

Tropical forests.

SIZE

60-143 pounds (27-65 kg), about 4.5 feet (1.4 m) long (the smallest of all bear species).

FOOD HABITS

Sun bears are primarily **vegetarian**, eating fruit, mushrooms, and honey. They eat some meat such as termites, lizards, frogs, and bees.

STATUS

The sun bear is an endangered species. It is hunted for its claws, skull, hide, meat, and gall bladder. People believe that because the sun bear appears to fall out of trees without being hurt, its body parts are capable of healing humans' bruises and broken bones. Special restaurants throughout Asia serve bear paws and meat to diners who think that a bear meal will give them good health. One bowl of bear paw soup costs several hundred American dollars! In addition, the bear's habitat is being destroyed as jungles are cleared for farms and homes. Early people believed that the markings on the sun bear's chest represented the rising sun. How sad that the sun may be setting on the survival of a species that we really never have known.

Sloth Bear *(Ursus ursinus)*

DISTRIBUTION

This bear lives in India, Sri Lanka, Nepal, Bangladesh, and maybe Bhutan.

HABITAT

Forests.

SIZE

120-300 pounds (80-125 kg), 4-6 feet (1.2-1.8 m) long.

FOOD HABITS

You might be tempted to call the sloth bear (pronounced "slow-th") the "vacuum bear." The structure of its nose, mouth, teeth, and lips forms a "sucking tube" that allows the bear to remove termites from their colonies. This shaggy bear also eats ants, honey, berries, and exotic fruits.

STATUS

The sloth bear is an endangered species. People hunt this bear because they believe the bear's body parts have magical powers. Destruction of the animal's habitat and poaching also threaten the animal's survival.

Asiatic Black Bear *(Ursus thibetanus)*

DISTRIBUTION

The Asiatic black bear lives throughout much of southern Asia.

HABITAT

Forested hills, mountains, and tropical forests.

SIZE

200-265 pounds (90-120 kg), 4-5 feet (1.2-1.5 m) long.

FOOD HABITS

The Asiatic black bear eats insects, honey, acorns and other nuts, fruits, berries, carrion, small mammals, grain, and in some countries, livestock.

STATUS

Except in a few areas, the future of the Asiatic black bear is bleak. In Japan the animal is regarded as a "pest" and can be killed at any time. People of China, Japan, and Korea favor this bear for medicine and cooking. Cubs are taken from the wild to be trained as circus performers. If conservation measures are not taken soon, the Asiatic black bear may become extinct in the near future.

The line that connects the Spirit Bear's mouth and heart is called a heartline. It is a symbol of the bear's power.

Spirit Bear

Design by artist Jean Bales of the Iowa tribe.

Spectacled Bear *(Tremarctos ornatus)*

DISTRIBUTION

The spectacled bear lives in the Andes Mountains and coastal foothills along the western part of South America.

HABITAT

Mountain forests.

SIZE

175-275 pounds (80-125 kg), 4-6 feet (1.2-1.8 m) long.

FOOD HABITS

The spectacled bear eats berries, fruits, figs, palm nuts, small mammals, birds, cattle, and corn.

STATUS

Killed for its body parts and deprived of habitat, the spectacled bear is a rare and endangered species. As few as 2,000 bears may live in the wild. Several zoos have begun captive breeding programs of these rare animals.

Giant Panda *(Ailuropoda melanoleuca)*

Some scientists place this bear in a separate family—*Ailuropodidac*—that evolved from true bears 18-25 million years ago.

DISTRIBUTION

The giant panda lives in China and Tibet.

HABITAT

Mountains in cold, damp bamboo forests.

SIZE

165-300 pounds (75-135 kg), 4-5 feet (1.2-1.5 m) long.

FOOD HABITS

The giant panda eats bamboo stems and leaves, other plants, and sometimes fish and rodents.

STATUS

An endangered species, fewer than 1,000 giant pandas currently survive in the wild. Because their habitat has been destroyed, giant pandas have become isolated on small wilderness "islands" surrounded by humans. Another threat to the giant pandas are traps set by poachers for musk deer. These snares often catch pandas instead. The extinction of the giant panda in the wild would be a loss not only to the children of China, but to the children of the world.

Bears of the World Map

The game includes:
- The "Bears of the World" map on pages 16 and 17
- The "Bears of the World" stickers in the center of the book
- The answer key on page 63

Before playing:
- Remove the section of stickers that shows the different species of bears.
- Notice how many stickers there are of a particular bear. You have many black bear stickers, but only a few sun bear stickers. The number of stickers will give you some idea of the population numbers of different bears.
- Read "Bears of the World" on pages 10 to 14.

Objective:
- To place bear stickers on the map to show where in the world each species of bear lives.

To play:
1. Study the world map on the following two pages.
2. Carefully remove one bear sticker. Find the species of bear in the information you have just read in "Bears of the World." Look under **DISTRIBUTION** to discover what continent the bear lives on, and what habitat is its home.
3. Look for the continent on the map, then look for the bear's habitat within that continent. Lick the sticker and put it in place.

After playing:
You will have stickers left over. Use one of each species of bear to decorate page 3 in this book. You may place other extra stickers in your favorite sticker collection book or share them with friends on letters or gifts.

The water pottery jar shows a bear paw design. Some Native American cultures believed that the sun's power flowed through the raised paws of the bear.

**Bear Paw
Water Jar**

Bears of the World Map

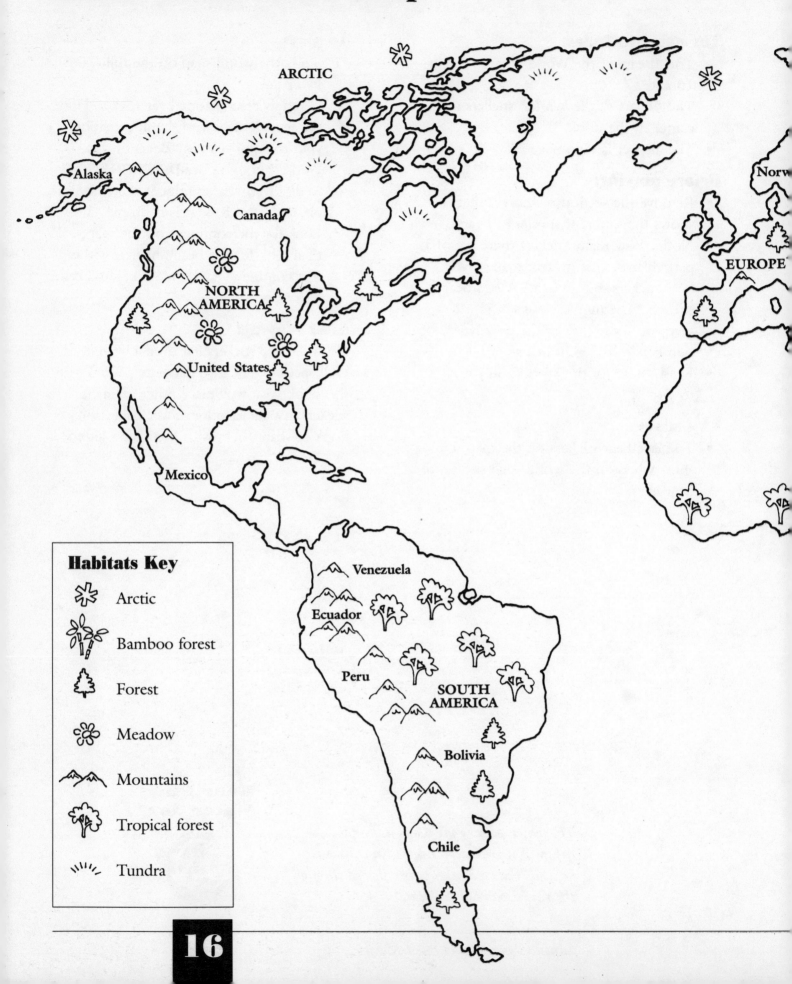

ARCTIC

Alaska

Canada

NORTH AMERICA

United States

Mexico

Norw

EUROPE

Venezuela

Ecuador

Peru

SOUTH AMERICA

Bolivia

Chile

Habitats Key

Arctic

Bamboo forest

Forest

Meadow

Mountains

Tropical forest

Tundra

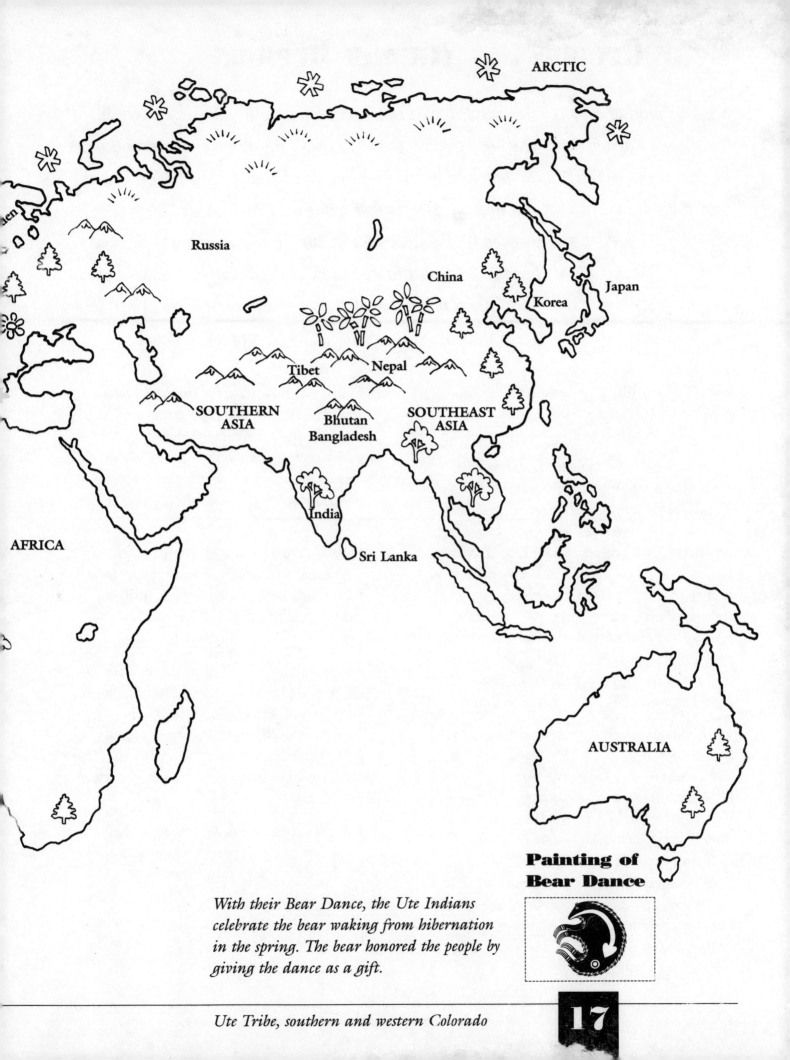

ARCTIC

Russia

China

Korea

Japan

Tibet   Nepal

SOUTHERN
ASIA   SOUTHEAST
         Bhutan   ASIA
      Bangladesh

India

AFRICA

Sri Lanka

AUSTRALIA

**Painting of
Bear Dance**

*With their Bear Dance, the Ute Indians
celebrate the bear waking from hibernation
in the spring. The bear honored the people by
giving the dance as a gift.*

Ute Tribe, southern and western Colorado

Bear Dreams . . . Human Dreams

Sus-ru's mother zips his silver jumpsuit so that it fits snugly under his chin.

She hands him a small white patch the size of a bandaid. The boy removes the strip from the sticky back and attaches the patch to his wrist. He immediately begins to feel warm and drowsy. His mother leans over and kisses him on the forehead. "We'll see you in our dreams, darling." With a faint smile on his face, Sus-ru closes his eyes. His mother and father apply the white squares to their own wrists, lie down in their capsule-shaped beds, and go to sleep.

The year is 2100. The world's ecological problems have been solved. The sky and water are clean and blue.

You may be wondering why. Scientists have solved the mystery of hibernation. Half of the world's population sleeps for six months each year. When the first half wakes up, the second half sleeps. Half the population requires fewer resources and less space. And sleeping humans remain in contact with active humans through their dreams. Is this science fiction? Yes, but only for now. Researchers are already exploring the possibility of hibernation for astronauts on long space voyages. Presently, humans cannot hibernate. But who can?

Ground squirrels, chipmunks, snakes, bats, and bears hibernate (except for sun, sloth, and panda bears). In "winter sleep," or **hibernation**, an animal's body temperature drops and its heart rate and breathing slow down. The heart rate of bears drops from about 40 beats per minute to 10. Their body temperature is lowered from 101-89° Fahrenheit (38-32°c). (Just for comparison, our heart rate is about 70 beats per minute and our body temperature, unless we are sick, is about 98.6°F [37°c].)

Bears may hibernate for three to seven months. During this time the animal does not eat, drink, urinate, or defecate. A person can live for only 40 days without food, and only four or five days without water. Imagine not going to the bathroom for six months!

How does a bear know when to hibernate? Researchers believe that shortage of food, severe weather, or a bear "that just cannot eat another bite," are all factors.

In northern climates, a black bear may den under a brush pile, dig out an area beneath a fallen log, or just settle in the middle of a laurel patch. Hollow trees are choice sites. In the Great Smoky Mountains National Park, black bears prefer the shelter of a large tree and will often dig out a space among its roots.

Grizzlies spend considerable time digging their dens with their long claws and powerful muscles. They often tunnel into a hillside, where the rock and dirt from their digging rolls down the slope. Some grizzlies have been known to move a ton of dirt while building their dens.

The grizzly prepares a small entrance, a tunnel, and a sleeping chamber. The sleeping chamber is just a little bigger than the bear—a smaller area holds heat better than a larger one.

Some people believe that bears sleep so soundly they cannot be aroused during hibernation. Researchers who have been treed by bears "exploding" from winter dens will tell you not to whistle your favorite tune in the ear of a hibernating grizzly bear.

Although bears mate in the late spring and early summer, the young are not born until the middle of winter. The cubs weigh less than a pound. This adaptation is important; large, active cubs would be difficult to manage in the close quarters of a den. Also, small nursing cubs do not stress the hibernating mother.

How does a bear prepare for hibernation? It eats and eats and eats! During the summer and fall, a bear may consume as many as 40,000 calories a day, and spend 20 hours a day eating. Grizzly bears have been known to accumulate eight inches of fat! This fat storage is critical. It allows the bear to hibernate and the mother to produce cubs.

What foods do black or grizzly bears eat when they come out of hibernation? You might think that a waking bear would eat everything in sight. However, the bear's digestive system does not begin functioning fully for about two weeks. Fortunately, healthy bears generally have fat reserves when they emerge from the den.

Bears are **opportunistic** and **omnivorous**. They will eat almost anything, plant or animal, that is available in their area during the season.

Plants can make up as much as 80 percent of a grizzly's diet in western North America. In the spring, grizzlies eat bison or elk that died during the winter. Grizzlies also will kill new calves and elk weakened by winter. As spring progresses the grizzly turns to grazing. Favorites are grasses, clover, dandelions, and biscuitroot. Throughout the summer ants, grasshoppers, and other insects are eaten in addition to small mammals such as marmots and voles. In summer bears move to areas where fish spawn. As berries ripen later in the summer, bears turn to this food source. Finally in the fall, the pine nuts become an important part of the bear's diet.

How could an understanding of hibernation help humans? A knowledge of hibernation could benefit astronauts in space travel. This state of deep sleep could be useful in surgery. During hibernation bears have high cholesterol levels, but they do not suffer from fatty build-up in their arteries—a condition that produces heart problems and strokes in humans.

In a sense, all of us are mini-hibernators. When we sleep at night our heart rate and breathing slow down, and for this short period we do not eat, drink, or go to the bathroom.

Under a crystal blue sky, Sus-ru skimmed along the sidewalk on his air-skates that automatically righted him if he lost his balance. His best friend waved to him from the corner. Sus-ru smiled in his sleep—it was only a dream.

Bear Dreams

Do bears dream when they hibernate? Just for fun, let's imagine that they do. On a separate piece of paper, draw what you think bears dream about when they hibernate. We asked children in Bozeman, Montana, and Denver, Colorado, to draw "bear dreams." Some of their pictures are shown below.

Gretchen's bear dreams about a cleaner environment.

Kelly's bear dreams about the beach.

Jessica's bear dreams she is a princess.

Cassandra's bear dreams there are forest fires.

Garrett's bear dreams about trading places with people.

Counting Calories

The game includes:
- The menu below

Before playing:
- Read "Bear Dreams...Human Dreams" on pages 18 to 20.

Objective:
- To see how much you would have to eat if you were going to hibernate like a bear.

To play:
1. Study the menu and choose your meal.
2. In the space below the menu, or on your own piece of paper, draw everything you want to eat.
3. Add up all your calories. Did you reach 40,000? If not, how much more would you have to eat?

COUNTING CALORIES MENU

APPLE PIE WITH ICE CREAM
one piece—400 calories
whole pie—3,200 calories

CHEESE PIZZA
two slices—400 calories
whole—2,400 calories

BARBEQUED RIBS
six ribs—250 calories
24 ribs—1,000 calories

BACON DOUBLE CHEESEBURGER
one—500 calories

BURRITO
one—400 calories
a dozen—4,800 calories

CARROTS, RAW
one—25 calories
a bag (about 20)—500 calories

BAKED POTATO
one large—100 calories

COLA
one can—150 calories
a six-pack—900 calories

CORN ON THE COB
one ear—100 calories
20 ears—2,000 calories

CREAM OF WHEAT
one bowl—100 calories
20 bowls—2,000 calories

SPAGHETTI
one cup—300 calories
one gallon—4,800 calories

FRIED EGG
one—100 calories
a dozen—1,200 calories

SPINACH
one cup—50 calories

EGGNOG
one cup—300 calories
one gallon—4,800 calories

HOT DOG
one—100 calories
one package (10)—1,000 calories

HOT CAKES WITH SYRUP AND BUTTER
three—500 calories

ICE CREAM
one scoop (large)—200 calories
20 scoops—4,000 calories

MARSHMALLOWS
one—25 calories
one bag—1,000 calories

CHOCOLATE MILK
one cup—200 calories
one gallon—3,200 calories

MILK SHAKE
one—400 calories

POPCORN
one cup—50 calories
one bag—700 calories

CELERY, RAW
one stalk—5 calories
one bunch—50 calories

RICE KRISPIES®
one bowl—200 calories
20 bowls—4,000 calories

MACARONI AND CHEESE
one cup—400 calories

CINNAMON TOAST
one slice—200 calories
a loaf of bread—3,000 calories

A Sleuth of Bears

Most of us enjoy a good mystery. As the detective uncovers the clues, we try to figure out who did it before the culprit is revealed.

In their study of the natural world, scientists use many of the same techniques as Nancy Drew and the Hardy Boys.

The power of observation and attention to detail are two qualities shared by criminal as well as natural detectives. Investigators also learn everything they possibly can about their subjects.

Bear researchers are truly "bear sleuths." After a radio-collared bear has been located, they hike into an area and analyze what the bear has been eating. To do this work, biologists must know what kinds of roots bears dig; their grazing habits; how they hunt gophers, ants, and other insects; and so forth.

Every good detective puts together a "dossier," or file, on his or her subject. The "Ursus Dossier" has been prepared for you. Study it carefully. Then using your powers of observation, solve the case!

URSUS DOSSIER

Classification

Bears are **mammals**. Like humans, they are **warm-blooded**; they generate their own body heat. Bears breathe air, nourish their young with milk, have backbones, and are covered with fur. The young are born alive. Young bears are nurtured and trained by their mothers for a long time. Some grizzly cubs have been known to den with their mothers for three years. All bears belong to the family, *Ursidae*.

Past Record

Bears and dogs share common ancestors. But about 38 million years ago, they began to follow different paths. About 4 million years ago, the first *Ursus* appeared in Europe. It was an ancestor to bears that followed. The size of a small bear, its features were different from the **canids**. Canids include dogs, wolves, and foxes.

Unlike canids, *Ursus minimus* walked on the soles of its feet. Like modern bears it was **plantigrade**. The bear's "insides" had changed. The gut was longer. An animal that eats plant material requires a longer gut because plant fiber is harder to digest than meat. Over millions of years the bear continued to evolve, retaining its **carnivorous** (meat-eating) past, but also adopting omnivorous (all foods) habits and traits.

The bear's teeth had changed as well. Unlike dogs or mountain lions which tear their food, bears crush and grind with their low, rounded **cusp** (the peak of the crown of the tooth).

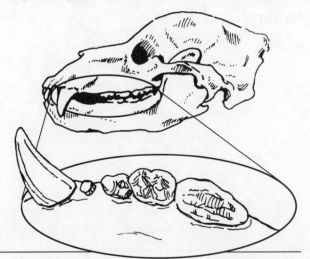

Senses

Bears have small, widely-spaced eyes. Up close their eyesight is good. For seeing long distances they sometimes stand on their hind legs. Bears have an excellent sense of smell. They can sense carrion (dead animals) miles away! Their hearing is good, much better than a human's, and similar to the range of a dog's.

Physical Characteristics

☑ Heavy-bodied with dense, long fur.

☑ Short, stubby tail.

☑ Short, powerful legs.

☑ Flat-footed walk (plantigrade).

☑ Five toes on each foot.

☑ Muscular hump (grizzly only).

Food Habits

Bears have powerful jaws with large canine teeth and smaller incisors for killing prey. But in the great survival game, bears improved their odds. They became omnivores, capable of eating a variety of foods.

Bears may delicately munch on berries, graze in a meadow, fish a salmon stream; steal whitebark pine nuts from a squirrel's **midden** (a squirrel's storage place), furiously dig up voles, rip apart tree stumps for insects, demolish beehives for honey (and bees), or take down an elk calf for meat. Of course bears differ in their food habits because they live in different places with varying climates and habitats.

Lifestyle

- Most bears are solitary. Bears in a group (for mating or when they are young) are called a **sleuth** of bears.

- Bears often mark trees with their claws, or use trees for scratching posts.

- Bears can be very fast. Over a short distance, a black bear or grizzly can run 25 miles an hour (40 km/h).

- A grizzly may live 15-20 years in the wild. A black bear may live for 15 years or more.

- A grizzly or black bear may rest during the heat of the day in a **daybed** (a shallow hole dug in the dirt).

- Bears (particularly grizzlies) have been known to follow the same trails—even placing their feet in the same tracks as bears that went before them.

- Bears enjoy swimming to relieve itching and to cool off.

- Bears seem to "play"—not only cubs, but also adults.

Buffalo Hide War Shield

The warrior who carried this buffalo hide war shield with its image of a bear sought the power of the bear to protect him in battle.

A Search for Suspects

The game includes:
- The "Ursus Dossier" on pages 22 to 23
- The scene on the next page
- The magnifying glass and the list of suspects on this page

You need:
- Scissors
- A pencil

Before playing:
- Read the "Ursus Dossier."
- Cut out the magnifying glass along the dashed lines.

Objective:
- To find clues in the scene that will help you identify the suspects that may have passed this way. The animals will not be visible—only the clues they left behind.

To play:
1. Use the magnifying glass to focus on small areas of the larger picture.
2. When you find evidence, trace the circle inside the magnifying glass around the clue.
3. List the clues you have discovered with the appropriate suspect. Some animals leave many clues, others very few. Some of your suspects may not have even been on the scene! Cross those suspects off your list.

After playing:
- Check the answer key on page 64.

LIST OF SUSPECTS

SUSPECT: **BIRD** _____

_____

SUSPECT: **ELEPHANT** _____

_____

SUSPECT: **FISH** _____

_____

SUSPECT: **GRIZZLY BEAR** _____

_____

SUSPECT: **HORSE** _____

_____

SUSPECT: **PERSON** _____

_____

SUSPECT: **RABBIT** _____

_____

SUSPECT: **SQUIRREL** _____

_____

Real Bears Don't Eat Marshmallows

"Excuse me," *the gray haired gentleman said to the woman in the gray and green uniform. "What have you done with all the bears?"*

Probably the most frequently asked question in Yellowstone and other "bear parks" is "Where can I see a bear?" People who visited Yellowstone before 1970 are often disappointed that they can no longer feed bears along the main park road.

During the 1930s, visitors could sit in grandstands and watch bears feeding on garbage. Throughout the park bears were eating at open dumps. The "no feeding of wild animals" policy was not strictly enforced. People were getting hurt, and bears who got into trouble were killed.

After researching the problem, park managers decided that bears and garbage were not a good mix. In 1970 the last park dump was closed. Visitors were better informed about not feeding bears and were fined if they insisted on tossing marshmallows from car windows. Bear-proof trash cans were installed.

Every effort is made to keep bears separate from human food. Today a visitor seeing a grizzly digging roots in a meadow is sharing an experience that connects him or her to early Native Americans and early pioneers and explorers. By eating roots, berries, and whitebark pine nuts, the bear is doing exactly what its ancestors did hundreds of years ago—being a real bear!

© Photo Archives Yellowstone National Park

The photographs in this album were taken in Yellowstone's early days. With the information that we have today, figure out what is wrong with these pictures.

Write captions for these old photographs to convince people that feeding bears is bad for both bears and people. You might want to make your point with humor.

When bears associate humans with food, conflicts can occur that result in the person being injured and the bear killed by managers. Many bears were killed in the days when these activities were allowed. If a mother bear ate junk food, she probably taught her cubs to do the same. The cub would probably get into trouble when it grew up.

The Three Bears

This game describes the food habits, dangers, activities, and encounters with humans in the life of a grizzly bear mother and her two cubs. As the mother and cubs emerge from their den they must make the proper choices to survive until the next denning up. They must avoid "population sinks."

What is a population sink?

Bear biologists describe a **population sink** as an area where bears and people come into contact. When a bear is attracted to a population sink and problems develop, it is either killed, sent to a zoo, or moved to a more isolated wilderness area.

The game includes:
- The game board on pages 30 to 31
- 2 mother bear and 4 bear cub playing pieces on page 33
- 12 fish food point tokens on page 33

You need:
- Crayons, color pencils, or fine tip markers
- Scissors
- Tape, paste, or glue

Before playing:
- Color, cut out, and assemble the playing pieces.
- Color and cut out the fish food points. Place them in a pile in the river on the game board.
- Read the directions on page 30.

Objectives:
1. To be the first player to move the mother bear and her two cubs to the opposite side of the board, and
2. To collect six food points.

"THE GRIZZLY'S LAST STAND"

© DMNH Photo Archives

This bronze statue of a mother grizzly bear and her two cubs can be seen at the Denver Museum of Natural History in Colorado. John A. McGuire, a Museum trustee, gave the Museum the statue in 1930. (A "trustee" belongs to a group of people who vote and make decisions about how the Museum will be managed.) As the publisher of *Outdoor Life* magazine, Mr. McGuire was concerned about the plight of the grizzly bear. His hope was that people viewing the statue would become more aware and, therefore, more involved with the future of this vanishing species.

The mother grizzly and her two cubs were models for the playing pieces for the game, "The Three Bears."

The Three Bears Game Board

To play:

1. Place the playing pieces anywhere in the first row on each side of the board.
2. Decide which player or players (teams of two may play against each other) go first.
3. You may move only one bear per turn.
4. The mother bear may move one or two spaces (word square or picture square) in any direction (forward, backward, sideways, or diagonal) in a straight line.
5. The cubs may move one space only, forward or sideways only.
6. The player who moves all three bears to the opposite side of the board and also has six food points in his or her possession wins! If bears have been lost along the way, the player that moves the most bears to the opposite side wins as long as he or she also has six food points. Therefore, a bear cannot den up until it has at least six food points. A player must stay "in play" on the board attempting to gather food points until he or she has six.
7. If a cub falls through a population sink, it is off the board. If a mother falls through a population sink, the player loses the game. (Cubs cannot survive if they are orphaned during their first year.)
8. If you are forced to land on a square that is already occupied by another bear (cub or adult), you must give up one food point to that bear. You remain on that square with the other bear, and ignore any directions written on it.
9. The winner must have six food points and be the first with the most bears on the opposite side of the board.

Wild strawberries. **COLLECT 1 FOOD POINT.**

You are radiocollared as part of a bear research program. **MOVE AHEAD 1 SPACE.**

Dig up family of v **COLLECT 1 FOOD POIN**

Hiker enters posted, closed area and you encounter him. **LOSE 1 TURN.**

Mountain lion! If mother is within 2 spaces of you, you're safe. **IF FURTHER, YOU'RE OFF THE BOARD.**

Camper leaves a dirty camp. You feed on hotdogs. **SINK!**

You slide down a snowbank—as you play, you learn. **TAKE EXTRA TURN.**

Campers leave co on picnic tabl You destroy it get to food. **SINK!**

Backcountry camper does not store food properly, and you feast. **LOSE 1 TURN.**

Motel owner feeds you garbage to entertain his guests. **SINK!**

Good trout fishing. **COLLECT 1 FOOD POINT.**

Good trout fishi **COLLECT 1 FOOD POIN**

Eagle! If mother is within 2 spaces of you, you're safe. **IF FURTHER, YOU'RE OFF THE BOARD.**

You encounter a bear-proof garbage can. **MOVE AHEAD 1 SPACE.**

TRASH

n approaches too
ely with camera.
her bluff-charges.
SINK!

her kills elk calf.
**COLLECT
OD POINT.**

Mother defends cubs
against large male bear.
**MOVE AHEAD
2 SPACES.**

Natural food is
scarce. Mother kills a
sheep from a poorly
tended flock.
SINK!

Coyote!
If mother is within
2 spaces of you, you're
safe. **IF FURTHER,
YOU'RE OFF THE
BOARD.**

Rest in daybed
near den.
LOSE 1 TURN.

Bison carcass.
**COLLECT
2 FOOD POINTS.**

You encounter a
poacher. Bear parts are
sold for medicine,
jewelry, and "magic."
**YOU'RE OFF THE
BOARD.**

Outfitter leaves a
dirty camp.
SINK!

Open garbage
dump on
the edge of town.
SINK!

Good meadow grazing.
**COLLECT
2 FOOD POINTS.**

For oil and gas
exploration new roads
criss cross habitat.
SINK!

Dry summer:
poor pine nut crop.
**MOVE BACK
2 SPACES.**

**COLLECT
1 FOOD POINT.**

Previous feeding area
has been logged.
SINK!

swim to cool off
relieve itching.
**VE AHEAD
1 SPACE.**

Cache of whitebark
pine nuts.
**COLLECT
1 FOOD POINT.**

Large male grizzly!
If mother is within
2 spaces of you, you're
safe. **IF FURTHER,
YOU'RE OFF THE
BOARD.**

Elk carcass.
**COLLECT
1 FOOD POINT.**

After playing:

When you have finished the game, place all the playing pieces and fish food points together in an envelope. Tape the envelope to this page so you can keep your playing pieces together to play again.

Bear Mother and Two Cubs

This section of a totem pole shows Bear Mother and her two cubs. In the legend, a woman marries Bear Man and they have twin cubs.

The Three Bears Playing Pieces

Remove this page from the book. Color one set of mother and cubs brown, the other black. Color the fish any way you like. Cut out the fish, then assemble your bear playing pieces.

To assemble the bears:
- Cut along the dashed lines.
- Fold along the solid lines so the side you colored faces out.
- Overlap the flaps to form a base and paste or tape.

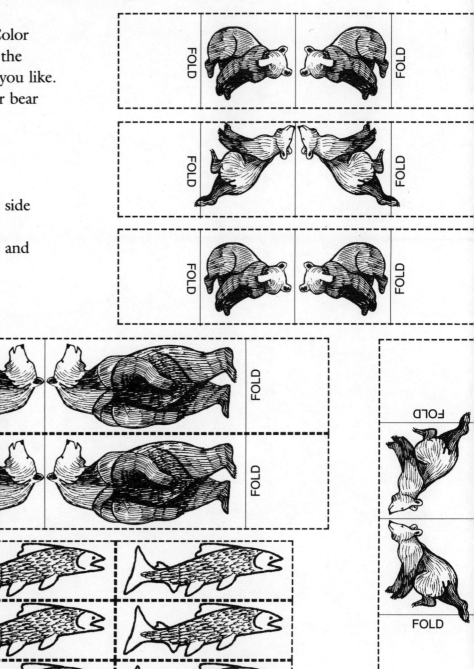

Somewhere for the Everywhere Bear

Gary Brown watched the two cubs and sow grizzly shake off the effects of the tranquilizing drug.

He was relieved that the **antidote** had brought them all around at the same time. If the mother came to before the cubs, she might wander off and leave them.

Gary looked at the meadow bursting with the colors of spring wildflowers. In the distance he could just make out the blue ribbon of a stream winding through a low, boggy area—good grizzly habitat. Far from hotels and cars and closed to hikers and fishermen, this bear management area would give the bears the chance they needed.

Coming out of hibernation the bears had been feeding in the southeastern part of Yellowstone National Park. But hikers, fishermen, and parties on horseback had displaced the bears. Bears are shy and will generally avoid humans if they can. But bears that are forced to leave feeding areas because of people may come into conflict with other bears. A mother grizzly must protect her cubs from other bears that will kill and eat them.

The mother had moved her cubs into an area where park visitors stayed in cabins, canoed, and picnicked. The fishing was good for people…and bears. Gary shook his head and smiled as he recalled the soggy fisherman. For unknown reasons, the mother grizzly had rushed up behind the fisherman, pushed him into the stream, jumped in after him, swam across to the other side, and began hunting for frogs.

When bears and humans come into conflict, bears must either be trapped and moved to a wilderness area, sent to a zoo, or in very serious incidents, killed. Using a culvert trap, rangers had captured the mother and two cubs. The three animals were transported by helicopter to this "bear management area."

A **bear management area** allows bears to live natural lives without being disturbed by humans. These areas are closed to all human activities (hiking, fishing, horseback riding, and so forth).

Gary Brown had been a park ranger for 37 years. He had seen too many incidents of bear-human conflict that ended with the bear being destroyed.

During the 1960s and early 1970s, he saw many problems. Bears fed at open dumps in the parks. Trash barrels were easily tipped over by bears. People freely fed bears and left food out in campgrounds. When the bears hurt someone, they were either trapped and moved, or killed by rangers. Gary concluded that the problem was not bears, but people.

When Gary went to work in Yellowstone in 1981 much progress had been made. Park dumps had been closed and bear-proof garbage cans had been installed.

But Gary was still not satisfied. Too many bear-human conflicts within the park had nothing to do with garbage, but with displaced bears or bears that were forced to compete with people for food or space. Gary felt that some areas of the park should be closed to people certain times of the year in order to give bears "space" for feeding, breeding, or traveling. These areas were called "bear management areas."

Today Gary is retired from the National Park Service, but he is not "retired" from bears. He has written a book, *Great Bear Almanac*, about his favorite animal. The book reflects his knowledge of and his love and respect for the great bear itself.

When asked how he felt about bears, Gary responded, "Bears are wilderness…they are the part of wilderness that has to be there in order to have a complete wild system….It won't be wild out there without them."

Gary says that he hopes never to see a world without bears. Because of his dedication, and sometimes just plain stubbornness in what he believed to be right, there is somewhere for the Everywhere Bear.

The Boy Who Lived with the Bears

by Sozap (Joseph Bruchac)

Native Americans have long believed that a special bond connected bears with people. Stories are told of humans marrying bears, or having a bear for a parent. Many traditional tales tell of people who have lived with bears.

One of the most common clans among native people is the Bear Clan. Such clans usually say that at least one of their ancestors was a bear.

"The Boy Who Lived with the Bears" is a popular story among many Indian nations of the northeast. Similar stories are found throughout the continent—from the Pueblo Indians of the southwest to the Athabascans of Alaska.

This is how the story goes.

Once there was a boy whose parents had died. Only his mother's brother was left to care for him. The uncle was a great hunter, but he thought the boy was a nuisance and did not treat him well. He gave the boy only scraps to eat and ragged clothing to wear. So it was that the people of the village called the boy Dirty Clothes.

Dirty Clothes, though, remembered what his parents had taught him. "Always respect your elders," they said, and so the boy did whatever his uncle told him to do. He hoped that one day his uncle's heart would soften toward him.

But as each day went by, the uncle grew more and more tired of caring for this troublesome boy. Then one morning, in the Moon of Flower, the uncle woke with an idea twisting in his mind.

"Today," the uncle said to himself, "I will rid myself of this useless boy." So he called the boy to him. "Come," he said, "today you will go hunting with me."

Dirty Clothes was very happy. It was the first time his uncle had ever taken him hunting. But as they started to leave the village, he noticed two strange things.

"Uncle," he said, "are you not taking your dog with you?"

"Today," the uncle said, "you will be my dog."

So Dirty Clothes followed his uncle into the forest. He did not ask his uncle about the second strange thing which was this. Always, when people left the village to hunt they went to the east or the south or the west. But today, Dirty Clothes and his uncle were going toward the north. It was said that strange things occurred in the forest to the north and so the hunters did not go that way.

Deeper into the forest they went until at last they came to a clearing. On its far side was a hill with a cave at its base.

"There are animals in that cave," said the uncle. "Crawl in and drive them out."

The cave was small and dark, but Dirty Clothes remembered what his parents had told him, "Always obey your elders." So he crawled into the cave. Deeper and deeper he crawled until he came to the end. There were no animals. He turned and began to crawl toward the circle of light which was the cave mouth. But as he approached it, the light suddenly went out. He crawled to the place where the light had been and found there a huge stone, wedged tightly. It was then he realized that his uncle wanted to get rid of him. He felt very sad, not only for himself, but also for his uncle, whose mind must be twisted to have done such a bad thing.

As the boy sat there in the dark, feeling alone and lonely, he began to remember a song his mother had taught him.

"Sing this song when you are feeling lonely," she told him. "It may help you to find a friend."

So the boy began to sing that song, softly at first and then louder.

> *"Wey-ah nah wey-ah nah wey-ah nah hey*
>
> *Wey-ah nah wey-ah nah wey-ah nah hey*
>
> *Wey-ah nah wey-ah nah wey-ah nah hey*
>
> *Wey-hey yo-oh-oh wey-hey yo."*

He sang the song again and again. As he sang, he thought he could hear other voices singing with him. He stopped singing and listened. Indeed, other voices were coming from outside the cave. But those voices were strange, not really like human voices. Then, suddenly, the voices stopped and the stone was rolled away.

The boy crawled out, blinking his eyes against the bright light. There, gathered in the clearing were all the animals of the forest.

"We have heard your song," they told him. "Do you need a friend?"

"I have no family," said the boy.

"Then choose from among us," said the animals.

So the boy listened to the animals tell him what their lives were like. None of them sounded right until the mother bear spoke.

"You would like to be a bear," she said. "We go through the woods and no other animal bothers us. We sleep in a warm cave. We eat berries and honey. And my two cubs will wrestle and play with you all day."

"I will be a bear!" said the boy.

So the Bear Boy went with his new family. It was as the mother bear said. He enjoyed being a bear. The mother bear treated him with great kindness and cared for him well. He forgot what it was like to be a lonely human. He wrestled and played with his new brothers. Each time they scratched him, black hair grew from his body. By the time it was the Moon when Salmon Spawn, Bear Boy was covered with black hair and looked like a bear.

Now the days were beginning to grow shorter. Then, one day as they went through the woods, the mother bear stopped.

"Listen," she said, "a hunter is in the woods."

The boy listened and he could hear the soft sound of feet, not two feet, not four feet, but two feet and four feet.

"It is Two Legs and Four Legs," said the mother bear. "We must run!"

Then she began to run. Bear Boy and his two brothers were close behind her. They ran through the forest, up and down the hills. But Two Legs and Four Legs were close behind. Bear Boy could hear the terrible cry of Four Legs coming closer. At last they came to a clearing where a big hollow tree lay on the ground.

"We must shelter in here," said the mother bear. And the four of them hid inside the tree.

Bear Boy heard Two Legs and Four Legs come into the clearing and approach the log. Then all grew quiet.

"Perhaps we are safe," he thought. Then he began to smell smoke. With the smell of smoke he remembered things he had forgotten. Two Legs and Four Legs were a hunter and his dog. And when a hunter wishes to drive a bear out of a log, he may make a fire to fill the log with smoke. Bear Boy remembered, too, that he had once been a human.

"Stop," he called out. "Do not harm my family."

The smoke stopped coming into the log. Bear Boy crawled out on his hands and knees, blinking his eyes against the light. There stood the hunter. It was his uncle.

The uncle stepped toward him and touched him. The hair fell from Bear Boy's body. He again looked like a human.

"My nephew," said the Uncle. "Is it truly you?"

"Yes," said the boy. "These bears are my family. They cared well for me when you threw me away. I will not let you harm them."

"No," said the uncle. "If they cared for you, then I shall treat them as my relatives, too. After leaving you in the cave, I returned to our lodge. As soon as I stepped inside, my mind grew clear again. I began to think straight. I hurried back to the cave to set you free and treat you as a relative should be treated. But you were gone and from the many footprints of animals about the clearing I thought you had been killed and eaten."

Then the uncle embraced Bear Boy. He treated the bears as he had promised. From that day on, Bear Boy and his uncle called themselves relatives of the bears, the first members of the Bear Clan. And they told this story, which has passed down from generation to generation, to remind grown-ups to always show their children as much love as can be found in the heart of a mother bear.

The End

Me and Bear

Hunters who have skinned a bear for the first time are often startled to recognize how similar a bear's anatomy is to a human's. We share several physical characteristics with bears. But Smokey Bear, Paddington® Bear, the Care Bears®, and our own teddy bears show us that we have very special feelings for bears. Do we see something of ourselves in bears?

Play "Me and Bear" in order to learn more about bears...and yourself.

The game includes:
- The "Bear Grid" on page 45
- 12 "Me and Bear" people cards on page 43
- Answer key on page 64

You need:
- Scissors
- A pencil

Objective:
1. To discover the similarities between bears and people by matching people cards to the bear grid, and
2. To make three matches in a row.

Before playing:
- Cut out the people cards on the next page.

To play:
1. Shuffle the cards and deal six cards to each player. Decide who goes first.
2. When it is your turn, look at the playing grid, and match one of the six people cards in your hand with the bear picture on the board. Be sure to read the information on the card out loud before you place it on the board. Some of the people cards have false statements. If the card is false, you may either discard it, or play it to block your opponent.
3. Only one people card can be placed on any bear space.
4. If you are the last player to put down the card that makes three in a row, you win that round, as long as all three cards are true statements. In order to win, there must be three correct matches. If you put down the last card in a row, and one was incorrect, you lose! Whoever wins two out of three games is the champ!

Bear Claw Necklace

The awesome power of the bear is represented by the bear claw, otter fur and bead necklace. Worn by honored warriors and Indian leaders in the midwest.

Me and Bear People Cards

1. Bears and people eat plants, so they have similar kinds of teeth—flat molars for grinding. The polar bear has sharp molars because it mainly eats meat.

2. Bears often stand on their hind legs to see things at a distance, to sniff, or to hear better.

3. The prints of an adult person and a bear show five toes, and are about the same size. Bears and people are **plantigrade**; they walk with the foot flat on the ground.

4. A bear track is deeper than a human track because bears are heavier than people. Humans and bears both walk on their toes.

5. Because they are mammals, bears and people share several characteristics. Their young feed on the mother's milk. They have hair. Bears and people are warmblooded.

6. The bear shows amazing skill in the use of its front paws. The bear uses its **non-retractable** claws as tools when digging roots, or as weapons for gripping prey. Young bears use their claws for scaling trees.

7. Bears and humans have similar needs: clean water, shelter, food, and "space." Because humans share these things with bears, no bear population is in trouble today.

8. Mother bears, particularly grizzlies, are very protective of their young. Human mothers share this maternal instinct.

9. Eating meat, fruits, and vegetable matter, bears and people are omnivores. In addition, bears also share people's love of "sweets."

10. Like humans, bears have **binocular vision**. Because the eyes are arranged close together in the front of the face, bears and humans can judge depth and distance. The ability to judge depth is important to a predator.

11. Humans and bears demonstrate great curiosity. In their search for something to eat, bears examine everything in their path.

12. Human mothers and bear mothers are very protective of their young. Like human children, bear cubs will stay with their mothers until they are ready to have their own families.

Me and Bear Grid

Twin bear cubs have been carved on this stone food bowl. In a legend the twin bear cubs are changed into humans, but retain their bear qualities and become great hunters.

Twin Bear Food Bowl

Tlingit, southern Alaska

Playing It Safe in Bear Country

Packing a bear pack

The best time to begin preparing for a trip into bear country is before you leave home.

Flares, signal mirrors, and a bright orange poncho are important in case of an emergency. A first-aid kit and the knowledge to use it are a must. Binoculars (for scanning the countryside for bears) and a flashlight (when you need to leave the tent at night) are very useful.

What information do you need?

Call ahead to the park or area where you will be hiking. Find out what kind of bears live in the area. Ask if there are any particular problems (such as bears that eat garbage).

When you arrive at the park

1. Read available pamphlets that provide information on hiking and camping in bear country.
2. Attend a naturalist program about bears. Ask questions!
3. In most national parks, you must register for a backcountry campsite.

Know the "signs"

1. Before entering bear country, note any special warnings posted at the trail head. If the area is closed, stay out! Otherwise, you will be endangering yourself and the bear.
2. Know the track, scat, and claw marks of the local bear species. Watch for carcasses, daybeds, or shredded stumps.
3. Be aware of your surroundings. Use common sense. If fish are spawning and you are walking beside a tumbling stream, recognize that bears will likely be feeding in the area. When you are in open country, use binoculars to scan the area for bears.
4. Make noise while walking through dense vegetation.

Pitching a tent in bear country

1. Cleanliness is probably your greatest protection when camping in bear country. Cook away from the area where you will be sleeping. Avoid cooking greasy foods, such as bacon, with odors that attract bears. Wash dishes and pots completely. Throw your dishwater far away from your sleeping area. Burn your garbage, or seal it in plastic bags and store it with your food cache, far away from where you sleep.
2. After supper, wash yourself and change into clothing that does not have cooking odors.
3. Always sleep in a tent in bear country! Set up your tent close to a tree with your head at the opening facing the tree. NEVER keep food of any kind in your tent.

What if...

What if you have done everything correctly, and you surprise a bear in the wild. In advance, think up a "plan," a kind of a mental "bear drill."

The following is a suggested course of action. But bears are intelligent and individual. For these two reasons alone, they are unpredictable.

1. Do not run! You cannot outrun a bear. The bear may stand up on its hind legs. This position is not an attack posture. The bear is deciding what to do.
2. Do not make eye contact, or any quick movements. Look around for a tree to climb that will get you at least 12 feet off of the ground. If you decide to climb a tree, drop something, such as your pack, that will distract the bear. Stay in the tree until you are certain the bear has left the area.
3. If there are no trees, and the bear doesn't appear to be particularly interested in you, you may be able to back quietly out of the area.

Shaman's Crown

This shaman's crown is made of bear claws. A shaman is a man who has special healing and spiritual powers. The bear spirit took away the shaman's fear of fire, and allowed him to walk across hot coals with no injury.

Tlingit, southern Alaska

4. If the bear growls, or "woofs," it is no longer just holding its ground. You are in danger. When the bear lays its ears back, you are probably going to be charged. However, it may be only a **bluff charge** where the bear will veer off at the last moment. If you are being charged by a brown bear, you probably have no option left but to curl up in a ball and "play dead." Protect the back of your neck with your hands, and lie still! The bear may sniff at you, even bat you around, but if you can refrain from yelling or struggling, it will likely lose interest and wander off. Be sure the bear is gone before you get up!

5. Black bears are usually tolerant of people, but they, too, can be dangerous. Your response depends upon where the attack occurs and the bear's behavior. For example, a black bear attack in a remote area can mean the bear is seeing you as prey. So you probably should not play dead. For more information on black bears and other bear attacks, read *Bear Attacks, Their Causes and Avoidance* by Stephen Herrero.

You probably will never have a problem with a bear in the backcountry. Most bears avoid people. But you are acting irresponsibly if you hike or live in bear country without knowing the facts or following common sense guidelines. The bear can only be a bear. We must protect both ourselves—and the bear.

Bear Totem Sculpture

This bear totem sculpture shows a bear holding a frog at its base, and a bear at the top. The bear is said to eat frogs.

Playing It Unsafe Cards

1. Tuck a candy bar in your sleeping bag. Bears cannot smell that well!

2. In stormy weather, it is okay to cook in your tent.

3. When you find your campsite, you also find bear scat that indicates a bear has been eating human food. You're tired. Don't worry. Set up camp.

4. It's too much trouble to store your food on the bear pole. Leave it by the tent door.

5. Bury your garbage in the backcountry. It's a hassle to carry it around. Bears will never find it.

6. Sleep under the stars—you will have a better chance of hearing and seeing a bear.

7. Leave garbage and leftovers behind. The bears will clean up your camp after you are gone.

8. Sleep with your food to prevent it from being stolen by bears.

9. People fishing or berry picking in bear country can relax their guard. Bears are not interested in these habitats or activities.

10. If you are hiking in the back-country and you run into a black bear, relax. They are very friendly toward humans.

11. If you see a bear by the roadside or in your camp-ground, feed it. The extra nutrition is healthy for bears.

12. If you are chased by a bear, run downhill—they cannot catch you.

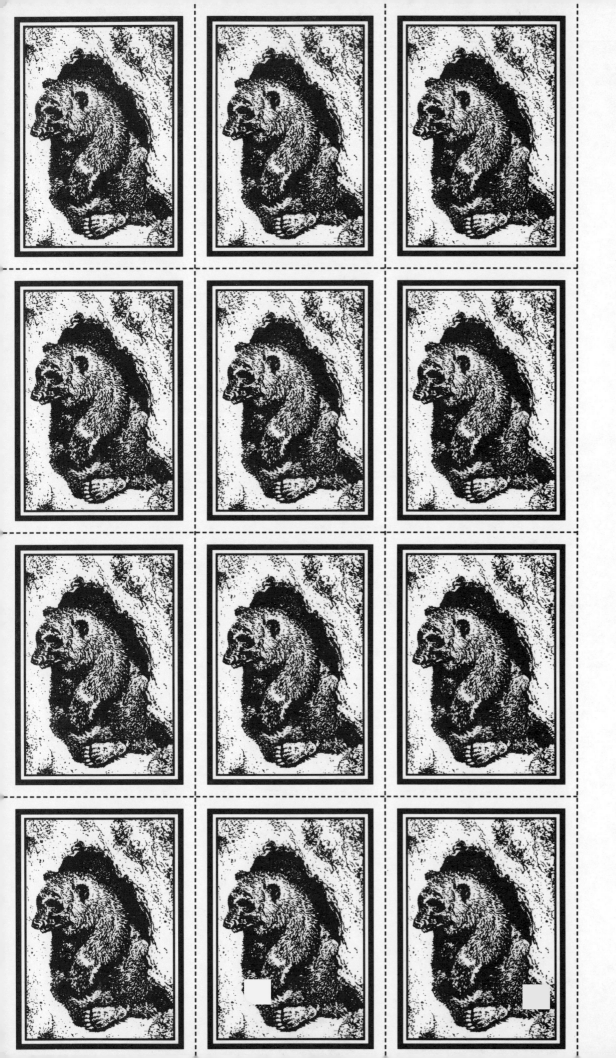

Playing It Safe Cards

Cut out these cards and the "Playing It Unsafe" cards and use them to play the "Playing It Safe" card game. Directions for play are on page 53.

Directions for play are on page 53.

1. Sleep in clothes that have not been worn while cooking.

2. If possible, camp in the open or near an "escape tree." Never put your tent in the middle or on the side of a trail through thick brush. The trail may be a bear highway.

3. A black bear usually can be chased away by shouting or banging pans together.

4. Cook at least 100 yards (the length of a football field) from your tent. Be sure the wind is carrying the food odors away from your sleeping area.

5. Leave your pack outside your tent (no food items) with the flaps open.

6. Properly store food at least 100 yards away from your camp.

7. In grizzly country, do not prepare foods with strong odors.

8. If there are no trees in the area, store your food in waterproof bags and submerge them in a nearby stream.

9. In **frontcountry campgrounds**, store food in the trunk of an automobile.

10. Horses and well-trained dogs usually provide early warning if a bear is in the area.

11. If you decide that climbing a tree provides a good escape route, be sure to climb high and fast. Some grizzlies have been known to scramble up trees to a height of 15 feet or more.

12. Bacon is not a great food to fix in grizzly country. Bears love its tantalizing odor.

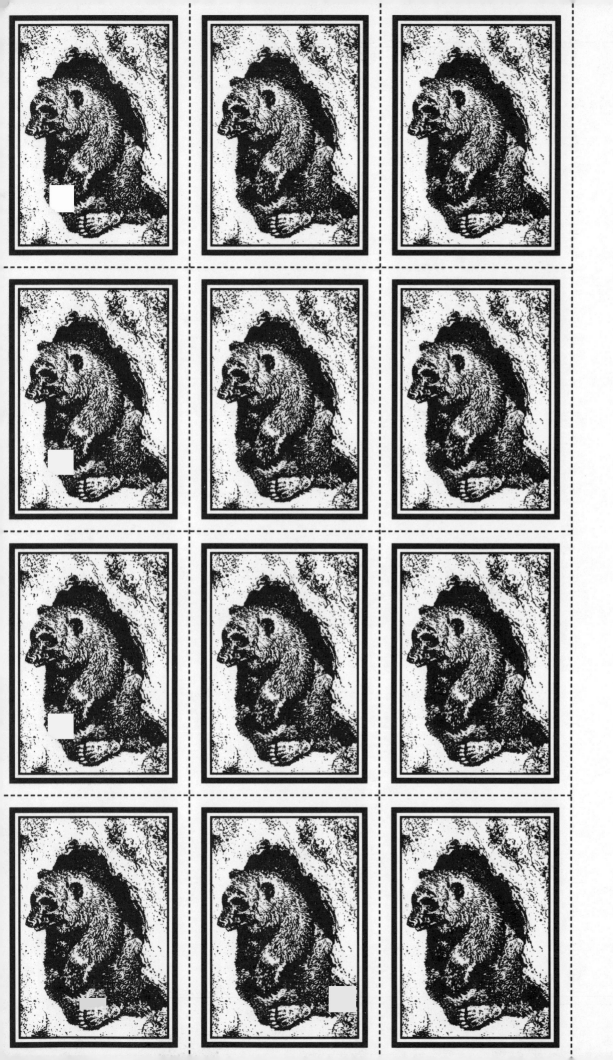

Playing It Safe Card Game

The game includes:
- "Playing It Safe" cards
- "Playing It Unsafe" cards
- Answer key on page 64

You need:
- Two sheets of 8 ½" x 11" paper

Before playing:
1. Make two tents following the directions below.
2. Cut out the "Playing It Safe" and "Playing It Unsafe" cards and shuffle them together. Place the cards in a pile with the picture facing up.

To play:
1. Take turns selecting a card. Read it out loud. If you think the card describes a safe practice, place it in your tent slot. If you think the practice is unsafe, place the card in a separate pile. Players may then choose from either stack of cards.
2. When players have gone through all of the cards, and are convinced they have selected all the safe practices, they must check their responses against the answer key.
3. The player with the most correct responses wins.

TENT ASSEMBLY

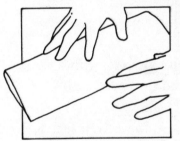

1. Fold 8 ½" x 11" paper in half, the long way.

2. Fold into three even panels.

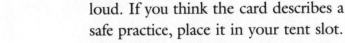

3. Unfold and lay flat. With scissors, cut from the top down to the first fold, and from the bottom up to the second fold.

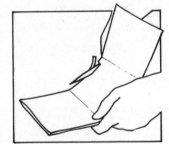

4. Fold in half again. Cut a slot in the center. Be careful not to cut too close to the cuts along the folds.

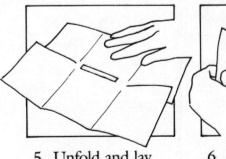

5. Unfold and lay flat again. Your paper should look like this!

6. Place the top left flap over the top right flap.

7. Fold the points down inside. Do the same thing on the other end.

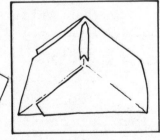

8. Turn it over. Your finished tent looks like this!

Playing It Safe Answer Key

PLAYING IT SAFE

1. Sleep in clothes that have not been worn while cooking.
2. If possible, camp in the open or near an "escape tree." Never put your tent in the middle or on the side of a trail through thick brush. The trail may be a bear highway.
3. A black bear usually can be chased away by shouting or banging pans together.
4. Cook at least 100 yards (the length of a football field) from your tent. Be sure the wind is carrying the food odors away from your sleeping area.
5. Leave your pack outside your tent (no food items) with the flaps open.
6. Properly store food at least 100 yards away from your camp.
7. In grizzly country, do not prepare foods with strong odors.
8. If there are no trees in the area, store your food in waterproof bags and submerge them in a nearby stream.
9. In frontcountry campgrounds, store food in the trunk of an automobile.
10. Horses and well-trained dogs usually provide early warning if a bear is in the area.
11. If you decide that climbing a tree provides a good escape route, be sure to climb high and fast. Some grizzlies have been known to scramble up trees to a height of 15 feet or more.
12. Bacon is not a great food to fix in grizzly country. Bears love its tantalizing odor.

PLAYING IT UNSAFE

1. Tuck a candy bar in your sleeping bag. Bears cannot smell that well!
2. In stormy weather, it is okay to cook in your tent.
3. When you find your campsite, you also find bear scat that indicates a bear has been eating human food. You're tired. Don't worry. Set up camp.
4. It's too much trouble to store your food on the bear pole. Leave it by the tent door.
5. Bury your garbage in the backcountry. It's a hassle to carry it around. Bears will never find it.
6. Sleep under the stars—you will have a better chance of hearing and seeing a bear.
7. Leave garbage and leftovers behind. The bears will clean up your camp after you are gone.
8. Sleep with your food to prevent it from being stolen by bears.
9. People fishing or berry picking in bear country can relax their guard. Bears are not interested in these habitats or activities.
10. If you are hiking in the backcountry and you run into a black bear, relax. They are very friendly toward humans.
11. If you see a bear by the roadside or in your campground, feed it. The extra nutrition is healthy for bears.
12. If you are chased by a bear, run downhill—they cannot catch you.

Ghost Bear

Wildlife photographer Stan Osolinski has photographed many species of animals all over the world. Whether slogging through snake- and alligator-inhabited swamps, or breaking through snowdrifts in sub-zero temperatures, he has done it all in high-top tennis shoes!

Stan went to Churchill, a small Canadian port, to photograph polar bears. In October and early November this small village bulges at the seams as 400 polar bears and large numbers of tourists "move in." What would a polar bear find interesting in Churchill?

Churchill is located on a large body of water that is frozen in the winter. During winter, polar bears are 40 to 150 miles out on the ice hunting seals. As winter turns to spring, the ice begins to break up into **floes** that the polar bears ride south. Finally the bears end up on the southern coast of Hudson Bay, and then move inland for the summer. As summer passes, the bears trek north so that when the ice freezes they can move out on the bay where the seals are. So, polar bears come to Churchill to wait…

"Hey, knock it off, get out of here, buddy—I came a long way to see this polar bear." Stan remembers his first view of a wild polar bear with mixed feelings. "It was dusk; we were just arriving in Churchill. We were on the outskirts of town, and there in the fading light I saw my first polar bear. At about the same time, a helicopter dropped out of the sky, and started dive-bombing the bear. The bear took a couple of swats at the annoying machine and ran away.

"I was really upset. Fuming I drove the rest of the way into town, and stopped to complain at the first place I saw." The local shopkeeper was apologetic, but said, "We must move the bears out of town. Tonight our children must be able to safely walk the streets." Seeing Stan's puzzled expression the man laughed, "You know, 'Trick or Treat'; it's Halloween!"

It was appropriate that Stan should see the polar bear on Halloween. Among its many names, the polar bear is also called ghost bear. In the days to come, Stan would understand the origin of this name. Photographing polar bears from the relative safety of tundra buggies, he observed polar bears who seemed to magically appear and then vanish in the swirling whiteness.

Stan witnessed the grace and beauty of the ice bears as they sparred and wrestled, and also their humor. "The ice freeze was really late; there wasn't much around for the waiting bears to eat. But they're resourceful. You'd see these bears drooling long strands of seaweed—kinda like green spaghetti."

Finally, when the weather has been cold enough long enough, the bay freezes and the waiting is over. Hungry polar bears then do what they do best—hunt seals!

Floe Facts

In some areas, to escape heat and insects, polar bears dig "summer dens." Some of these dens have been used for hundreds of years.

Used as paddles, the bear's front feet have webbing between the toes. The back feet steer the bear as it swims.

Serious threats to polar bears include oil exploration, offshore drilling, and oil transport through polar seas. Because oil is difficult to clean up, an oil spill in the Arctic would be disastrous.

On land and sea the ice bear is a tireless traveler. Polar bears have been found swimming 80 miles from land.

Sometimes a bear waits patiently by a breathing hole until a seal surfaces for a breath and the bear seizes it. Or the bear may swim, crawl, or creep to stalk its prey.

For hibernation, pregnant females build a "maternity den" that looks like an Eskimo igloo.

Born blind, deaf, and unable to smell or walk, cubs can see and hear within one month. The mother digs the family out of their den in March or April when the cubs are three to four months old.

Polar bear cubs weigh about 1 ½ pounds at birth. Although they are born in a snow cave, they have a very sparse coat. They stay warm nestled in their mother's fur.

Polar bear hair is clear and hollow. It gives the animal buoyancy in water.

Except for brief periods in bad weather or times of little food, male bears, nonpregnant females, and females without cubs do not hibernate.

Eskimos respect and often imitate the ways of the polar bear. Eskimos have many "spiritual obligations" when they kill a polar bear. They give gifts to appease it.

Polar bear leftovers are food for Arctic foxes, ravens and gulls.

With their heavy coats, sometimes bears become too hot. Excess heat is given off through footpads, claws, and other parts of the body. Bears will jump into Arctic waters and eat snow to cool themselves. Brr!

Polar bears can live to be 30 years old.

The bottoms of the polar bear's feet are covered with coarse fur so that the bear has traction on ice and snow.

Walrus Ivory Bear

This scene is carved from the ivory tusk of a walrus. It shows the bear and eskimo as hunters of a common prey—the seal between them.

Arctic Activities

Eskimos and polar bears have adapted to the harsh conditions of the Arctic. To endure long, dark, cold days, Eskimos played many different games.

Boys and girls had "snow knives." Made from wood, bone, or ivory, children used these knives to cut pictures in snow, mud, or dirt, and then tell a story about their drawings.

Another game, played with something that looked like a beanbag, was called "Catch the Bag." The bag was actually sealskin filled with sand. It was tossed from person to person. Anyone who failed to catch the bag was out of the game.

With your parents or friends read "Floe Facts" on pages 56 and 57. Find a ball, beanbag, a wadded up piece of paper—anything you can throw safely. Sit opposite your parents or friends. Toss the ball back and forth. If a player drops the ball, in order to stay in the game he or she must repeat one piece of polar bear information from "Floe Facts." The information does not have to be the entire floe fact, just a portion. Before the game can continue, players must agree that the fact is correct. If there is a dispute, check the book. The same fact can be said only once. Players are out if they miss the ball and can no longer recall a fact.

Ask a parent if you can have a plastic knife for your "snow knife," or just use a stick. (You may want to decorate your knife by drawing an animal on the handle.) Make up a fictional story about polar bears ("I will never forget last Halloween I met a Ghost Bear…"). Or, drawing in snow or dirt, tell the story of the bears of Churchill to your parents or classmates.

© DMNH Photo Archives

Eskimo print titled "Inuit Fishing as Three Bears Approach" and the snow knife shown above are from the Anthropology collection of the Denver Museum of Natural History.

Everywhere Bear: The Movie

Where is the Everywhere Bear going? Follow the directions below to make the movie. After assembling and viewing the movie, write a script to tell your own story about the Everywhere Bear. On another piece of paper you can make more filmstrips about the Everywhere Bear, or tell other stories.

The game includes:

- The filmstrip and screen below

You need:

- Crayons, color pencils, or fine tip markers
- Scissors
- Paste or glue, and tape

To assemble:

1. Remove this page and color. Then cut out the pieces along the dashed lines. Cut slots in the screen along the dashed lines.

2. Make the screen by folding along the solid lines with the type facing out. Paste the tabs matching **X**s to **O**s. You now have a box with one side open.

3. Thread the filmstrip from inside, through the slots, over the screen. Check to be sure the pictures face out. Tape the filmstrip together matching **X**s to **O**s. Run your movie by pulling the filmstrip around.

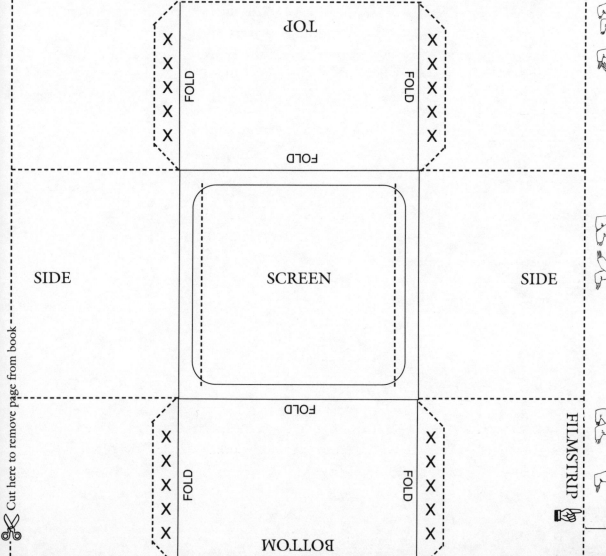

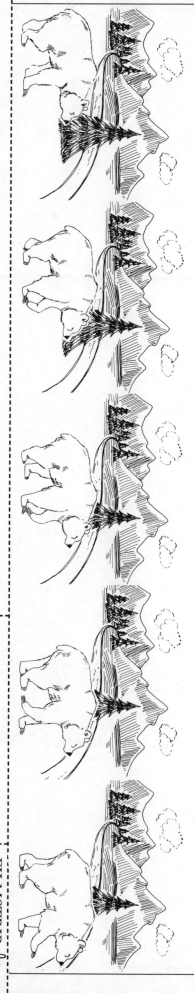

○ ○ ○ ○ ○   ○ ○ ○ ○ ○

○ ○ ○ ○ ○   ○ ○ ○ ○ ○

○ ○ ○ ○ ○ ○ ○ ○ ○ ○

Glossary

antidote (ANT-ih-doht)—a drug that counteracts, or works against, another drug.

baleen (buh-LEEN)—also called whalebone. This material makes up hundreds of thin plates that hang from the upper jaw of some whales. As water flows past these plates, the whale's food is filtered.

bear management area (BEHR MAN-ihj-mehnt AR-ee-uh)—an area in which bears are allowed to live natural lives without being disturbed by humans.

binocular vision (beye-NAHK-yuh-luhr VIZH-uhn)—vision that results when the eyes are arranged close together in front of the face, allowing for distance and depth perception.

bluff charge (BLUHF CHAHRJ)—a charge in which the bear veers off at the last minute.

canids (KAN-ihds)—relatives of dogs, wolves, or foxes.

carnivorous (kahr-NIHV-uh-ruhs)—an animal whose diet is made up almost completely of meat.

carrion (KAR-ee-uhn)—dead animals.

daybed (DAY-behd)—a shallow hole dug in the dirt in which a bear rests during the day.

digitigrade (DIHJ-iht-ih-grayd)—walking on the digits or toes of the foot, like horses.

floe (FLOH)—a large, flat piece of ice that separated from an ice mass.

frontcountry campground (FRUHNT-kuhn-tree KAMP-graund)—a campground that can be accessed by automobile.

habitat (HAB-ih-tat)—the place where an animal lives, an animal's home.

hibernation (heye-behr-NAY-shuhn)—"winter sleep"—a condition in which an animal's body temperature drops and its heart rate and breathing slow down.

mammal (MAM-uhl)—an animal that is warm-blooded, breathes air, nourishes its young with milk, has a backbone, and is covered with fur.

midden (MIHD-uhn)—the place under a tree where a squirrel stores food.

non-retractable (claws) (nahn-ree-TRAK-tuh-buhl)—the condition of not being able to draw the claws into pockets in the feet.

omnivorous (ahm-NIHV-uh-ruhs)—an animal that will eat almost anything, plant or animal.

opportunistic (ahp-uhr-tyoo-NIHS-tihk)—taking advantage of situations that are favorable to an individual.

plantigrade (PLANT-uh-grayd)—an animal that walks on the soles of its feet.

population sink (pahp-yuh-LAY-shuhn SIHNK)—an area where bears and people come into contact.

sleuth (SLOOTH)—a group of young bears that gather for mating.

vegetarian (vehj-uh-TEHR-ee-uhn)—an animal that eats only plant material.

Bibliography

Books

Bauer, Erwin A. 1985. *Bears in Their World*. Outdoor Life Books, New York.

Burch, Ernest S. 1988. *The Eskimos*. University of Oklahoma Press, Norman.

Craighead, Frank C., Jr. 1979. *Track of the Grizzly*. Sierra Club, San Francisco.

Domico, Terry. 1988. *Bears of the World*. Facts On File, New York.

East, Ben. 1977. *Bears*. Outdoor Life Crown Publishers, Inc., New York.

Herrero, Stephen. 1985. *Bear Attacks: Their Causes and Avoidance*. Nick Lyons Books, New York.

Lopez, Barry. 1986. *Arctic Dreams*. Charles Scribner's Sons, New York.

McGuire, Bob. 1983. *Black Bears*. Bowhunting Productions, Tennessee.

McNamee, Thomas. 1984. *The Grizzly Bear*. Alfred A. Knopf, New York.

Millen, Nina. 1943. *Children's Games from Many Lands*. Friendship Press, New York.

Mills, Enos A. 1919. *The Grizzly*. Comstock Editions, Sausalito, California.

Patent, Dorothy Hinshaw. 1987. *The Way of the Grizzly*. Clarion Books, New York.

Pfeffer, Pierre. 1985. *Bears, Big and Little*. Young Discovery Library, New York.

Rockwell, David. 1991. *Giving Voice to Bear*. Roberts Rinehart Publishers. Niwot, Colorado.

Schullery, Paul. 1986. *The Bears of Yellowstone*. Roberts Rinehart Publishers. Niwot, Colorado.

Servheen, Christopher. 1989. *The Status and Conservation of the Bears of the World*. Eighth International Conference on Bear Research and Management, Monograph Series No. 2.

Shepard, Paul and Barry Sanders. 1985. *The Sacred Paw*. Viking Press, New York.

Whitfield, Dr. Philip. 1978. *The Hunters*. Simon and Schuster, New York.

Interviews:

Gary Brown, former Bear Management Specialist, Yellowstone National Park (October 1991)

Jeff Henry, bear researcher and wildlife photographer (October 1991)

Stan Osolinski, wildlife photographer (November 1991)

Whale Baleen Basket

Alaskan eskimos believed that the bear spirit protected them from polar bears. The basket is made of baleen, also called whalebone, and the carved bear is ivory.

Answer Key

Nowhere For the Everywhere Bear Puzzle

Bears of the World Map

American Black Bear: Forests and meadows in Canada, Mexico, and United States.

Grizzly Bear: Tundra, forests, meadows, and coastlines in western North America.

Kodiak Bear: Alaska.

Polar Bear: The Arctic.

Sun Bear: Tropical forest in southeast Asia.

Sloth Bear: Forests in India, Sri Lanka, Nepal, Bangladesh, and Bhutan.

Asiatic Black Bear: Mountains and tropical forests in southern Asia.

Spectacled Bear: Mountain forests in South America.

Giant Panda: Bamboo forests in China and Tibet.

Artifact Stickers

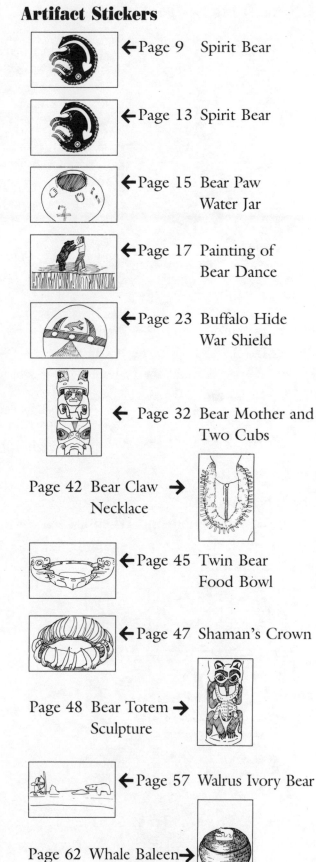

← Page 9   Spirit Bear

← Page 13 Spirit Bear

← Page 15 Bear Paw Water Jar

← Page 17 Painting of Bear Dance

← Page 23 Buffalo Hide War Shield

← Page 32 Bear Mother and Two Cubs

Page 42 Bear Claw Necklace →

← Page 45 Twin Bear Food Bowl

← Page 47 Shaman's Crown

Page 48 Bear Totem Sculpture →

← Page 57 Walrus Ivory Bear

Page 62 Whale Baleen Basket →

Answer Key

A Search for Suspects

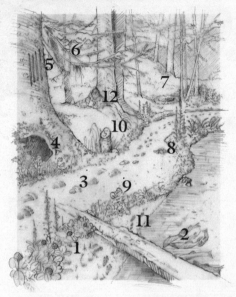

BIRD: **1**) tracks; FISH: **2**) in stream;
GRIZZLY BEAR: **3**) tracks, **4**) den,
5) claw marks, **6**) hair, **7**) daybed, **8**) scat;
PERSON: **9**) can, **10**) trail marker;
RABBIT: **11**) tracks;
SQUIRREL: **12**) midden.

Me and Bear

Check below to make sure your three in a
row are all true statements. When laid on
the Bear grid, the correct placement of
people cards looks like this:

1. True; 2. True; 3. True; 4. False;
5. True; 6. True; 7. False; 8. True;
9. True; 10. True; 11. True; 12. False.

Acknowledgements

The Denver Museum of Natural History
appreciates the encouragement, time, and
support of the following:

Project Sponsor—Valerie Gates Pettit

Publication Coordinator—Betsy R. Armstrong

Technical and Educational Review—Dr. Carron
Meaney, Dr. Elaine Anderson, Betsy Webb,
Joyce Herold, Michelle Conger, Leslie
Newell, Karen Nein, and Diana Lee Crew,
Denver Museum of Natural History.

Design—Gail Kohler Opsahl

Illustration—Marjorie C. Leggitt, Nancy
Malick, Gail Kohler Opsahl, Kay Herndon,
and Jesse Drost

Cover Illustration—Ann W. Douden

Art Production—J. Keith Abernathy

Special thanks to Chris Meyer's fourth grade
class from Graland Country Day School,
Susan Lipstein's class from Hackberry
Elementary School, and Alana Berland,
Katie Duffy, Whitney Frick, Jessica Harvey,
Colin Hudon, Jennifer and Jeremy Kamlett,
Heidi Lit, Adele Martin, Joe and Matt
McConaty, Erik Robins, Paige Stapp, and
Chad Spurway who tested the activities.

Cover illustration derived from photos by
Shattil/Rozinski.

Artifacts featured on the stickers are from the
Anthropology collection of the Denver
Museum of Natural History, and are on
display in the Crane Indian Hall on the
second floor.